A LAST LOOK BACK

ISBN: 979-8-218-24540-5

Peter Weltner was raised in suburban New Jersey and piedmont North Carolina, received his A.B. from Hamilton College and his Ph.D. from Indiana University, taught in the English Department from San Francisco State for thirty-seven year, and has published three novels, four collections of short stories, and twenty or so books of poetry, most recently *Sleeper, Waking* (Marrowstone Press, Seattle) and *Crow-Black Stones and a Flock of Crows* (Agenda Editions, UK,) and *A Last Hike In* (Marrowstone Press, Seattle) He lives in the Outerlands of San Francisco by the Pacific with his husband of thirty seven years, Atticus Carr.

A LAST LOOK BACK
Poems, New and Retrieved

PETER WELTNER

MARROWSTONE PRESS

Table of Contents

I.

I

Water Carrier

1.

It is possible the quest for meaning begins, in mythology
at least, when King Gilgamesh of Uruk wanders in search
of what he longs for most, first love, then immortality.

When the friend he's fought, then embraced has died, it's the sea
he seeks instead, diving beneath it as deep as he can go to reach
bottom, to dig in mud and uproot the plant that is rumored to be

his salvation. But all he discovers is the futility
of possessing it since the fateful, inalterable breach
between him and the gods remains, robbed as he is of eternity,

left forlorn like Achilles, after Briseis is taken from him to deny
him the spoils of war, wailing, lamenting on a windy beach
to his sea nymph mother, if he must die, let him be remembered for his glory.

2.

Lord Ea, initiator of poets, water-god, form-giver,
patron of artists, culture-shaper,
bearer of transient, flowing things, rain-maker,

dweller in the sky's seas with whale and fish and river
swimming above the earth, below it inhabiter
of the currents that flood the world when you are angry, dweller

in wells and streams and cisterns, the cosmic source for the water
living things require to survive, protector, giver
of life, are you not also, in another guise, Ganymede, cup-bearer

to Zeus, wafted to his palace on eagle's wings, the god's lover,
the handsome boy who pours wine into Zeus' golden vessel as the order
of the world is transfigured when love's seed flows from the younger into the older?

1

3.

A poem is not a well-wrought urn, a sealed or locked chest,
but a vessel to hold meanings whose expressive powers
are born from the wine or waters that flow into and out of it. Like a rest-

less, steady stream of stars or of rivers on earth, it is a metaphysical test
of permanence since poems often last no longer than flowers
whenever a thunderstorm rages. Or they might be suppressed

by time or authority, never to be discovered or quickly forgotten. None can wrest
the sense of words on their own since meaning is not ours
to define by ourselves. What words, metaphors, images, rhythms suggest

is inspired by the vessel they are poured into and out of, possessed
of the form they assume in the urn the water-bearer carries before he showers
its powers upon those eager to drink of it, like communicants in a rite of the blest.

4.

The milky way is a hundred billion stars—or many
more—unfathomable light years far
from earth. Near shore, waves throw foamy,

luminescent crests across a darkening sky. The sea
refracts their light like a prism. Close by, myriad tiny lights are
tossed still higher by crashing breakers, forming a galaxy

briefly risen out of the ocean, a constellation (say, a ram's head, eye sockets empty,
curved horns like Aries) spied in the moon-enflamed mist over tar
black waves rolling in. The water jets so high into the air it's as if the sea

itself is sparkling, glittering, offering a glimpse of the world's propensity
for poetry, pinprick droplets splashing, flickering star-
like, sparks flashing, expiring, each burst of whitewater beautifully, explosively fiery.

5.

An old, magic-minded poet is connecting verbal dots on a page, as if each one
he connects to the next might create an image, define
this line or that line, or realize a new figure, metaphor, or surprising design

as he begins to solve the puzzle. When done,
he hopes to find it is a poem, like a pitcher filled in
with water or wine, the points of light so intricately linked they align

with the configurations and names of constellations
through which eternal night rolls on
and on, as season

follows season and sun
and moon move into a different sign
that now is Ea's, water-bearer, urn-carrier, maker of poetry, cup and portion.

6.

Again, a late winter storm out of the west breaks into night
rattling windows, shaking trees, washing much of the beach
away or onto the dunes. I want to say to you it is all right
to be afraid of dark, unknown things sometimes. I want to beseech

you, too, not to fear how our lives ahead, now we've grown old together,
might turn meaningless. Do you remember how, long ago, you counted
in the constellation of Aquarius the number
of its stars you could name, interested not because they predicted

anything, but because after the night's cleansing storm they shone
even brighter in the sky than you'd ever seen them
before, the silence that followed after the winds had blown
themselves out like the stillness in a church after the singing of a hymn?

Mightn't it be true that rain releases, frees the heavens by falling, filling the sea,
spilling onto earth what the sun will drink when it shines again? Weather,
rain or shine, is ours to cherish. What does it mean to say one has had a happy
life? Look to the sky, back to the past. Oh, my love, when I am thirsty, you bring me
    water.

The Way Is like Valley Streams Flowing into Rivers and Seas

1.

Crossing borders, a bold enemy horde splashes
through gorges faster, more turbulent than
spring-stricken, white water spills and crashes
over rocks. A weary man sits on a cliff, no plan
in mind save to observe life's slow unfolding
and play the lute lying in his lap, its strings
untuned, its bowl warped. The world is going
mad, he thinks. Sorrows fill the songs he sings
deep in a forest too dark for battles. Shadows
at dusk from Pine Cone Mountain blacken the valley
below. Bitter is the wine he drinks, the blows
that have struck him all his life, bitter the day
the wars resumed, bitter the rice that tastes
of the dust horses' hooves leave swirling behind them.

A full moon gradually rises as cypress trees' stems
and needles weave together their delicate
threads of light and dark. In the river far
below, a boy lies asleep in his skiff. It's too late
to reach where he was going, safe from war.
The man picks up his lute and begins to strum
a song he used to sing when, young, he wooed
his love in a garden's midnight shade and hum
to the tuneful notes he plucked. How he begged
his mistress to be true, to be kind, to return:
the knot-haired, rice-powdered woman he loved.
The boy's boat floats buoyed by moonlight the river
reflects, a placid stream now, but soon to twist and churn
in the rapids pounding boulders with the clashing sounds of seas to come.

2.

Not absence. There's nothing mystical to discover
in this scene, no metaphysical silence to penetrate
within it. A moon over a sinuous river white water
white, but quiet, an ungraspable purity to it like the late

spring blossoms of magnolia and tulip trees along
its banks, moonlight seeping through the bristling
branches like mist, like wisps of fog, like a song
of nighttime's shining on a young man's dreams, an old man's longings.

A Last Look Back

I.

1.

Mt. Tamalpais,
too green for Greece yet
god-lit,

a dream of a strange peace
on fire in the sunset
behind it,

a goat cart
in my ears as I watch
children play-

ing at the start
of evening, two boys catch-
ing in their hands the last light of day.

2.

Wind-, fog-drenched, not rain
but mist dazzling, cool-
ing late morning,

a beach where, see, again
boys like us in a tide pool
idly wading.

3.

Summer weather
in Carolina fifty five
years ago,

or today, here, where it is hotter,
less clear, alive
with tourists, no

thunderstorms mid-afternoon,
no fireflies
at evening

as at twilight back home, we two laughing,
counting how many, your sighs
more joyful than anything.

4.

Like wind to sails, blue
skies to sun, boys as young
as we, not yet men,

concealing nothing, yet not quite true
either, speechless, like a tongue
on fire with all it burns unspoken.

5.

Your skin after swimming like oil
on a naked wrestler
in heroic Greece,

youth unspoiled
by fear. The epic matter
of hair like gold fleece.

6.

Though no Greek poet,
of course, I would pray
to the sea,

horizon, unbroken
sky, "May you stay
forever by me."

7.

Waves unerringly
roar, the Pacific I
walk beside

daily, ocean older than memory
now at its highest
known tide,

a sea ancient as Homer's, no
less wild, vast,
dangerous to

voyage on, to be betrayed by: not you
but him, long ago, racing through rain
to someone new.

8.

Whoever catches the bright glances
flashing from Theoxenus'
eyes

is tossed into the wild seas
of his desire (discus
thrower, gymnast). Whoever denies

his infatuation, that he dreams
night and day of him
has a heart of stone,

adamant as iron, how he gleams
with oil, like a hymn
to a god I wrote, bereft, alone,

you might remember, his Dorian
sandels fitted for
the everlasting dance of splendor,

like the garlands placed on Theron's
royal brow, to adore
him solely, olive shoots for crown.

II.

1.

Gray as wet rocks, clouds hang heavy
in the sky.
A surprising summer rain is falling.
Who I

am is an old man standing at the edge of a world.
The Pacific's
too wild for surfers today, shining
like a mix

of chrome plate and steel. A fisherman
in waist-high
waders is drenched by waves as he casts his line.
Why

must I leave you and the earth I love? In flocks,
pelicans,
their beaks like awls, fly south over
Land's End.

2.

When I was a child, I nailed
an owl's wings
found in woods to a plank I hung on a wall.
Such things

boys do unknowing of death, the stink, the look
of it,
its feathers rusting like fallen petals or leaves.
I sit

on a stone wall while a ship dredges the ocean
floor
for sand, loading itself with it like a barge
to restore

the beaches last spring's late storms washed
away.
Riptides along the shoreline are leaving a snake's
wavy

patterns on the sand. New driftwood lies by dunes
like bones
from a desert dig. A retriever runs loose, barks,
as if it owns

the coast, the gulls, ravens, plovers, the ball
its human
throws again. My father would feed the birds once winter
began,

suet, seed. Titmice, thrushes, finches,
chickadees,

cardinals. The shells they scattered on snow
were pleas

for more, darkly sparkling like pebbles seen lying beneath
a white sea.
A man wearing plugs in his earlobes,
ratty

cut-offs paws like a dog in the sand for something
he's lost.
A pit-black freighter, loaded with cargo, slips
like a ghost

ship out of the bay into a shroud of distant fog
and disappears.
My friend, here, where a continent finishes its journey,
here's

where we'll complete what remains of our days.   I am the lake
I swam in
as a boy, the ocean by which I walk each morning,
the din

of the surf I sleep to at night, the water
I've dreamed of
throughout my life, praying something of us might stay
like our love

for each other after we've died. I'm looking back
to a river,
flooded, overflowing its banks as sunlight
in summer

exceeds every measure, as migrating birds by their flying
empty
the sky, the sea, you, me of all but their flight's
fleet beauty.

Rocks and Stones

1.

Like love, form rises out of water like rocks in a Zen garden.
What ritual led them to be placed unplanned, yet exactly
there? Luck or artistry? No clocks, computers, no geometry
can make more rational a world into which all things
have been thrown or scattered. Chance mocks us, too,
and the truly rational might stand astride the earth,
laughing at our folly, the world too old to be told what
is unreasonable. No hands arranged these rocks, placed
just barely at the edge of the ebbing tide on the beach.
Each might be a character in a shadow play, the sky at dusk
like a painted backdrop, a cipher standing for empty space,
stones and rocks and pebbles sea-soaked to a calligraphic black.
Can lives be hidden, immortalized in stones? Design, happenstance:

neither is the answer. Form rises out of water like rocks in a Zen garden.

2.

At the beach, the air smells saltier
after afternoon showers. Rocks, stones,
pebbles tossed on sand by cresting tides
warm and dry in the heat. An otter
courts a shier, thinner one that hides
behind a boulder shaped like pine cones
jutting into the Pacific. It is miraculous,
this shoreline, as if spared all fault,
purified by sun and ocean, wind and rain.
To delight in tides and currents, to exalt
in a twilit sky as clouds drift away, crane-
white and feathery, is to be, in a way, religious:
pebbles, stones, rocks glittering in an evening sun,
waiting to be reclaimed by far-off seas, untamed and profound.

Sun and Moon

1.

The sun dazzles even through a scrim of clouds
like a god's piercing eye gazing down
on a small island town
where the old live, the unplowed,
infertile earth around it mainly rocks,
olive trees, flowering vines,
and scrub bushes. No signs
of youth remain, no clocks
to strike time's passage, to say what age
it is. The people here adore
their gods, slaughter goats, burn oil, pour
wine in their rites. They inhabit ancient memories
like stories alive today, the island still a landing stage
for the Delian League while triremes clash in far-flung seas.

2.

Water. Night. No godlier a good.
An island moon-drenched,
stucco white, bleached,
bougainvillea scarlet as blood.

Sleepless in bed. The sound of feet
on bricks and stones, birds
on tile roofs, small herds
of goats and sheep, the bleat

of one lost. Moonlight colder
than winter, than youthful
fires recalled, the dull
ache of failed love to remember,

dimmer than anything seen in the dark,
the misty mountains, the beach,
and all blurred, the search
suspended till day. A lone dog barks,

howls at the moon, icy white
the whole long night
it shines through windows
casting shadows,

wave-like and cresting. No godlier
a good, the ancients say,
than moonlight on water
showing lost sailors the way.

Consecration

Let noon consecrate the sky. Let light seep into caves
and cling, throw no shadows anywhere. Perched crows
mock a snub-nosed monkey while a kite braves

a spectacled cobra basking in the sun. A wind blows
more heat from fires in the east. A monk sits on
a hill overlooking a gorge in which a river flows

over rocks. He sips rice wine. No battle is ever won.
He mumbles an old poem about a drunken moon
and a white crane flying over a mulberry tree, a ghost-son

of the sky, maybe, or a buddha. A lark, a swallow, a loon
soar overhead. Women are threshing in the valley.
No dawn can come too late for them, no dusk too soon.
On western hills, their men die bravely in the ancient storied ways.

Boy with Kite

Twin mountains in the long domed shape
of spruce cones like those inscribed
on age-old screens loom over a landscape
like a scene on which has been painted,
in black ink, a flat boat two men pole
up a narrow, winding river, a deer herd
gazing out of piney woods, a speckled bird,
ducks, feathers wet, floating downstream.
High up, there's a clearing, a wood hut,
a pebbled path, a blossoming chestnut
tree a man sits under, cross-legged, robes white,
meditating or sleeping in a real, if dream-
like place where peonies bloom ageless as a scroll's
and a boy, while his dog traces scents, flies his paper kite.

Sonata in B flat minor

Whirlwinds, storms of notes blowing through the soul
near nighttime, sun slowly sinking, a half rainbow
arcing westward in the aftermath of winter rains.
Mortality is a wolf in the White Forest, an army
besieging Warsaw's gates. Wagtails, a wood warbler,
keepers of secrets, waxwings, thrushes spirited
into sight by chance of wind. A hearth fire's damp logs
crack and sparkle. Smoke-gray clouds are fired by
twilight: coal-ember-ashen, then char-black after the sun has set
into the Crooked Woods or Solska Forest where the endless sleep begins.

And so he dreams, dreams incessantly because his
soul is always Poland, the dance he is dancing
as he lies in bed at night, coughing,
the rains falling too late, the bliss
of fresh air to breathe, precious as a forest
in the homeland, as the aristocratic ball-
rooms of a livelier era, his lungs sorest
as he composes, beating time, in thrall
to his music's evocations of the sight
of a beautiful girl he had loved young lying
beside him deep in woods they had fled
to past barns, pigsties, wheat fields at night
in the days of the persecutions when rebels bled
and Poland danced to the mazurka in the mansions of the dead.

Fantasie in C major

Call it folly, the seasonal elation, the soulful irruption of fall's fauvist colors
as they catch fire, begin to blaze. Pine, fir, spruce resinous in the heavy air.
The lucidity of dusk's reign gathers, spills over the hills. A forest floor's
needles, moss, and ferns glow iridescent as batlight. A golden mist. What you'd dare
in the dark if you could. Polish the clouds' quicksilver shine. Embrace an empty moon.

Call it madness, love's nocturnal passion. Dismiss it as romanticism. How night
lingers, suspended in the sky. Autumn is the season of dying, they say,
of flying away. Two lovers depart by a bend in the road. It is not right,
it is not just they separate. Yet, look, the trees are unleaving faster each day,
white hairs grow whiter, and the sun nearing the horizon untethers itself from noon.

Sagaland

Strong as horses' haunches, wind-whipped,
North Sea waves race to shore,
surging like a groundswell or Norsemen
invading the land, bearing shields and swords.

Storms, icy rains toss thrashing bodies like boats
against rocks. The shoreline is stark
as a desert, treeless, desolate, its inlets
hidden by mounting piles of stones and scarp.

Many a black, jagged promontory juts
into the shrouded, gauzy, dun gray
sea, its swirling crests, spindrift brittle,
white as ice, cracking, splitting, fracturing.

Slowly, the land collapses into the churning
water like a body of mountainous
matter succumbing to its great weight,
too grievous for the earth to bear forever.

Sunlight lingers through each night like a Viking
ship set on fire, its hero and his golden hoard
burning cold-hearted and bloody as the winter
moon, steady as she goes, eternally mans its oars.

A Lone Old Tree on a Windy Hill

Once there was a sky refulgent with an inner light for the last
time that shone on a tree whose petal-like, crystalline, rime-
white leaves, trunk's gnarled, bony fingers grasped
at heaven as if the venerable, slanting, grassy earth was past

reviving it, though each leaf flowered, gleamed with a glassy,
milky glow. No skittish squirrels would try to climb
its coarse, blackened bark, no birds perch in it. Yet gladly,
sweetly flocks of rooks and starlings circled above it, sublime

in their ease, gliding and wheeling about it in leisurely
flight as if waiting for evening, each lovely, softly
cawing, clicking, wheezing, human-like note
they sounded into the surrounding night entreating it

to comfort them in the greater dark to come. Once there was a tree
devoted life-long to the birds and clouds that floated
over it, rooted on a windy, sloping hill until it grew too weary,
in its final luminous end-of-life-leafing, to survive alone, old and soul-lit.

Fog over Ocean Beach

The sea and sky are one today, gray gray gray,
shiny steel, burnished pewter, dull tin, lead,
weathered iron, the wide beach the gritty gray
of sidewalk cement pocked with black silken
threads of stuff tossed up by waves from ocean
floors and drowned logs and limbs cast ashore
by wild waves in last week's storms. Paddling out,
surfers vanish from sight into the gray unmarked
horizon, hikers walking north along the tideline
fading into the mist. This is the art of anonymity,
like letters written but never read or books graying

from years of dust unopened on a shelf. When the sun
rises high and hot enough to burn off the mist,
it will be like a projector light enflaming the film
it is showing, as if the screen on which the movie
was being seen had ignited, a black hole burned
through it until the lights in the theater are turned
on for those viewing it to leave safely, dissatisfied,
angry perhaps that they will never know how it ended
while after they've gone home the theater's lights will be
extinguished once more, the house left empty and sad and dark
as its gray silvery screen glows on and on though no one is watching.

Valentine's Day Dawns on the Outside Lands

The morning sun rises over a tranquil sea
shown in a painterly light, headlands
outlined with tight, incisive strokes, precise
as an etching's. Though it is February,
it might be spring already, sunrise free
of rain clouds, the sea pale and lambent
as the sky's translucent cerulean blue.

Miles away, near the horizon, the water
deepens into a viridescent, garnet-hued
ultramarine, its shiny, slick intensity
subdued by fog. The night before, hours
after sunset, the Pacific erupted
in rage, waves crashing on the beach
too fiercely for anything, even stones

or driftwood to know any peace. Cold winds
howled against hills, cliffs, walls, and parapets,
slashing through the park, snapping trees,
whirling leaves, pounding houses, demanding
to be let in. Now as late dawn pacifies,
lightly warms the eastern hill's jagged,
sharp, stark ridges, nothing stirs, not yet,

gulls, crows, pelicans perched on poles
or sea walls waiting to fly free, huddled
tightly together as if praying for the sun
to awaken them to the new day's
miraculous light, eloquent, kind as that
by which the saint brought his brutal
jailer's blind daughter to see and be healed.

Pacific Vigil

1.

Your ship sailed past here on its way to take
on soldiers and cargo. The pier's pilings rise
out of a fog-thick mist that, like this night, tries
to fool us with its calm. Streetlights make
a ghostly light, phosphorescent, lit from within.
At the western edge of the pier, no men wait
for departure, fearful, anxious about what fate
awaits them in the war. So let the stories begin,
tales of voyaging, of journeying to better worlds,
told to make the future less dreadful. I peer deep
into the sea, then turn around. As if asleep,
I'm dreaming a dream of you I repeat like words
of a prayer. I thought I might see you again tonight
while a worm moon seeps through clouds, then out of sight.

2.

Early the next morning, migrating pelicans,
a few geese, some plovers, a tribe
of white and gray gulls stay to feed
by the shoreline on tiny fish the tide

brings in. The sea is calmer after
days of rough currents and high waves.
Some sleekly feathered, bolder geese
swim or float in the water as in

a pond while pelicans circle above them,
their long, wide wings rarely flapping,
gliding in strong winds, their beaks
like slightly curved, thin scissors blades.

Most of the others seem to be waiting,
patient as birds carved from wood,
as if after such a feast they must take
leave of this beach and fly far off.

I would say they are staring out to sea.
I would say they are observing a rite
unknown to humanity. Like a prayer,
perhaps, or some way of offering thanks.

People walking their dogs off leash
pay them no mind, let them run
where they will, playing, barking, chasing
after, pursuing their elusive prey.

Like one, the excited birds soar off
in a roar of flapping like a gust of wind
from a sudden storm, disappearing
northward to some place we'll never see,

you and I, like a fantasy, a dream we held dear
fading into the sky. Like you.
Like the beach we made love on
before my fears grew too clear to believe in it anymore.

3.

Now the rain is falling harder, flooding gutters,
creeks, overflowing streams, and I
getting wetter while staring at the water
where I see you slowly, strongly, boldly

stroking, swimmer, spillway, bird wing,
moccasin, defiant, reckless despite
the charge in the sky, the deluge swamping
the earth, the sea, the risk, the thrill of lightning

striking the Pacific, throbbing air,
thunderbolts, rushing water,
crashing, gale-like winds: a vision not of despair
but the joys of lovers who have never been happier.

4.

I keep my promised vigil by walking each night by the sea,
gazing at its vast, anonymous graveyard,
grieving like a widow
whose husband drowned off this coast years ago,
wondering what he or I
or anyone might say to others knowing
death will touch them soon,
this afternoon perhaps,
what it might mean to ask
of your friends before you die
who will survive you,
to give them the task,
or maybe the favor
of transforming mourning into liturgy
as Jesus at his seder did,
requesting they eat bread, drink wine
in memory of me,
he said
as if any of them could forget
the death he gave them, the life they'd lost.

5.

Come. Grip my hand.
Let us leave this land.
Nothing ours may stand,

Waves beat fast,
cities fall, bombs blast,
fire rages. Let's find some peace at last.

Walk to the end of the dock with me. I'll say,
"Wars rule each day
of our lives. We can't stay

here." So we stare beyond night,
beyond moonlight,
beyond wrong and right

until like wind to sails, blue
skies to sun, boys still young
to wise old men,

at the mere sight of you
again, my tongue
will be tied, and all I meant to say left unspoken.

Moonlight on Sutro Heights

A strong ocean wind blows over Sutro
Heights, the ruins of a parapet,
the beach, the Great Highway far below
it, sea's waves too wild for surfers. Sunset
will arrive as soon as the fog drifts in,
clouding the Pacific. The horizon
early in December is a thin
line of gray like that of polished flat stone.
Sparrows sweep through wind-bent pines,
chirping noisily. The steep cliff
drops two hundred feet. The world seems full of signs
or ciphers like a newly found hieroglyph
illegible, inscrutable as the mist obscuring the city,
darkening the sea in its radical estrangement

from the dying calm of late fall, broken by the strangeness
of its depths' torments, its beautiful, senseless,
rare splendors. This morning after several days of rain,
the storm's strongest winds collapsed when the sun rose
and spilled over the highest hills,
though straying, wispy clouds still
shadowed the sleeping city. Like a middle west plain,
the sea was level as slate, rippled by low waves. Cattails, reeds
along the shoreline glistened in the murky water
flowing from the highway where rivulets and creeks
had formed from the runoff that cluttered the gutters.
At noon, a gray-green, coppery sea cast a sheen like a cat's amber
eyes, sparkling when sun struck. And now, transfigured by night, Sutro Heights
glows, too, its sheer escarpment white and flat as an iced-over lake in late winter.

A Last Sunday in June

Seventeen pelicans fly through dense fog in a line
straight as the horizon's. Dozens
of geese-making their ritual sign
of V across the sky, dark and small as wrens

to the eye where they glide far from the beach
over the sea, flock after flock-are heading
south this late in the season. Why? To reach
what feeding ground? And what makes them swing

round suddenly, as if they've decided to go back
to where they'd flown from earlier this morning,
then swirl southward again—like men trying to track
their traces when lost, frantic, worried—circling

round and round until each flock, one by one,
vanishes into the fog bank, out of sight.
It's low tide. Two men, glad not to be alone,
stand on a rippled tidal flat, holding each other tight.

Perhaps they hear in the air nothing strange, nothing
foreboding, just sea-music lulling them
to sleep some day soon as they listen to it sing,
its familiar melodies, steady beats comforting as a hymn.

Their eyes, their half-shut lovely
eyes, might seek, as lovers
sometimes do, the other's face, hoping to see
or find at last in each other some sign of a final rescue

from anguish and trouble. Seen from cliffs overlooking
the beach, the ocean is gray as the gentle rain
which has been falling lightly on everything,
soft as the dew of dawn that Isaiah said gives birth to departed spirits.

2.

"There's been nothing like this in the world before," one says.
"Some day the beach will be crowded with beautiful
people again, girls and boys, tourists, locals

enticed here by balmy, clear, perfect, safe summer days,
the water warm, the waves calm and embracing. A gull
will glide over two kids tossing their yellow beach ball

as a man rubs sun lotion on his boyfriend's shoulders. And the bay-
shaped cove between the cliffs that hide it, curved like a ship's hull,
will call us back to make love there as we did summers before the plague."

And then the two men, mere phantoms anyway, ephemeral visions
the ocean conjures when it's shrouded by mist, will swiftly vanish
like the pelicans and geese into the fog, into the hazy confusions
of lives unable to stay here flying, free as birds, to wherever they'd loved and played.

Dry Spell

The lore of shriveling woods, trees' leafless limbs
mingling, stretching skyward through pine,
live oak, the sweet, acrid odor of ripe persimmon
rotting on the forest floor, a hobbled fox
preying on rabbits, squirrels that lie
like carnage waiting for a predator to find them
already dead by a pond unfed by creek or stream,

the legends of clouds floating over cliffs and rocky
hillsides precarious to climb, geese flying
in flocks swiftly over continents faster
than wasps through a breezeway, a ledge
hikers climb toward a cave hidden behind
a tangle of ivy and vines, the darkness
inside it somnolent, unspoken, and cold:

these are the untold tales of the soul, of its dying,
ritualized into a struck bell reverberating into
silence in a temple where priests chant
prayers soft as birdsong heard in solitude
or the murmurs of a garden well after fall's
long dry spell, the echo resounding in it of leaves'
voices in the wind, brittle from drought, thirsty for rain.

Night Hunter Woods

A vole dangles from an owl's beak
until the owl devours it whole,
excreting beside a meandering creek
what little remains of it, the soul
of the furry creature lost forever
while the owl goes on the prowl
again, the quiet woods night-hunter
dark. Insatiate, it perches in an old-
growth oak, its bark gray, roots fungus
pocked. The whims of autumn, less cold
than winter, slyly predict its first light
snowfall will show nothing momentous
save for what still lies, exposed, on the newly white
forest floor: a vole's bony slivers bleached whiter by an owl.

Hoh River Valley

A chill winter mist sifts through trees in the pale
play of early morning light. Moss
dangles from branches and limbs along a trail
like long grizzled beards crisscrossing,
weaving through the forest.
Big leafed maples, sitka spruce
scary, shaggy as giant primeval
people who would dance sun-blessed
by dawn while antlered like elk, moose
furry in woods before the universal
cold descended and froze them into
ghostly poses, now shed only dew-like tears
unable to weep as they used to do
when they were human grieving at the oldest of their fears.

Fire Pit

The usual white-capped waves roll in more gently this morning,
the sea in its far westerly reaches emblazoned by
the sun, like a field of freshly fallen snow mirroring
a light so blazingly white it blinds the eye
to gaze at it. A crowd of elderly men and women
has gathered at ocean's edge, stretching their arms
out to the horizon, bowing to the surf. I try to listen
to their chanting but don't understand it. What harms
might their beliefs inflict on others, I wonder. Fires burn
in pits surrounded by bricks. They're seeing something
I cannot see, believe in gods or powers I'd think deluded,
irrational, no doubt. What is there, if anything, to learn
from rites and myths others keep faith in? What's enlightening
about ways of being from which all your life you've been excluded?
If the earth is not holy it must die. If the sea is not sacred it means nothing.

Palinode

1.

To write on water, in air,
to watch every leaf
decay, disappear
in winter, to despair

past enduring in the belief
of anything's lasting,
to dare to write nothing
from fear

the words that once proved of use
are false as faith, to care
for reality
more than the lies

of a poetry
that dies
from abuse
by aspiring to immortality,

to want to say goodbye
not knowing
how to say it, the world too dear
to deny

it: so bends the tree
to earth,
the flower rises to the sky,
from birth

to death the river
flows, water
to water, the city
builds its cemeteries,

history
is written
as the tragedies
of unwise lives,

and heaven
is seen as a dream best dreamed by
children.
How bear it then,

the cry
you listen
to in the night and choose
not to hear

when there's still much to lose?
People ruined, nations rent
by wars, pestilent
politics. And language left desolate

inert, silent before suffering,
the child in the tenement
stairwell begging,
the soldier in the desert

dying, a battered wife. It's too late
for poety.
Attain stillness.
Embrace emptiness.

Drift on an ocean, blown about endlessly.

2.

I believed, reasonably, that the antique-looking cast iron frying pan
I cooked with each night was the one my grandmother had used
and her grandmother before her, belonging to a world older than
I could ever know until my husband reminded me he'd bought it. I refused

to admit at first it had been his gift only two decades ago. But it's true.
My grandmother's cookware hides in the cluttered back of a cabinet
in our kitchen crowded with things I've forgotten, couldn't say to you
how many if forced to. How much of memory is desire haunted, beset

by confusion and mistakes? I haven't much time to learn left to me.
I wait for peace like everyone else. I fear a future of untold diseases.
I long for a world that is older than it is and wiser, for art and poetry
and music to matter importantly again. I want to do whatever pleases

the gods I never knew and could not have known. I wait for the Dharma Wheel
to revolve, to turn once more, for Jesus to come back. I want some poem
to save me, though I'm sure none can. I want reality. I want to do real
things, not trust in words or the mysteries of dreams or visions. I want to say 'home.'

3.

Nothing living–whether wild or tame, enchained or free,
well-fed or hungry, safely settled in country or in towns or cities,
whether wandering over land or roaming freer by air or sea–
nothing, no one is spared mortality's
power despite what artifacts say, what monuments
proudly display. Even poetry is only a passing reminder
of what once was, a sign of what the human spirit invents
that for a while helps us to remember,
the past like conjurers of spells, like magicians
evoking restorative visions or a longed for story,

like that morning when the sea's breezes where I lived were as saltily
sweet as the incense of smoldering rose wood and posterity, glory
were the sky's opening to the sun as meadows of wild black-eyed susans
and Wood's blue asters unfurled to dawn with the world's recurrent,
vivid, briefly lived, wordless poetry, as if this were the sense of it when all goes silent.

Birch Forest

Wide fields white as the long beards of Russian monks,
shadows black as the cassocks of old believers,
the early morning light flickering off the icy trunks
of birches, their brittle leaves like candles on altars
in a dimly lit church flittering off the dulled gold
of icons, lake and creeks frozen hard as the hearts
of proud infidels or doubters: a forest like that told
of in tale by a Slavic writer, by a map that charts
the path we took through a curvy wooded trail,
rutted, slick with black ice, old oaks fat as oxen,
fallen limbs, stumps, boles gray as the bits of shale
scattered everywhere, noon bright enough to frighten
wolves in a world as numbed as this was that long winter
day faith failed us, both of us lost in our wilderness together.

Ox-Head Road

Bells slowly retreat back into silence
in a temple where monks murmur
prayers. A river, in the absence
of rain, flows past soft as a whisper.

It is rumored flowers thrive for a century
or longer along Ox-Head Road
repeatedly blossoming, their beauty
as deathless as sculpted images. The load

of human suffering is too heavy for anyone
to bear alone. It is uncanny how trees see
people with leaves' eyes, stones
and rocks know their secrets, birds pacify

them with their songs, how plants with thorns
understand them. Though monks hang
scrolls on temple walls, what truly mourns
for the dead? Who rings a bell as once it rang?

Look. As the sun slips behind a mountain,
glutted hawks soar toward
heaven, and priests pray for rain,
for the thousand years of peace to be restored

that ghosts might fly again over Ox-Head Road,
their crow-like spirits invisible to us all,
though the lake they seek is shadow-flamed like the unsowed
fields where they perch in trees cracking seeds and caw and call.

E and O: Heron

Suppose Orpheus and Eurydice returned
from the land of the dead (composed
of forbidding furies, yes, but also blessed
spirits, for this is Gluck we are listening
to in the Age of Enlightenment) to find
that they had been changed into a bird,
a heron, standing on a water and wind
striated rock like the pinnacle of a very
high mountain, below them a wisp of a sea
so calm it appears to be a lake in winter
or clouds obscuring the rest of the range
and the earth far below and everything
otherwise white in the purity and simplicity
of light and the air, the air, the brilliancy
of air they can breathe in again, and take wing
in: what then?

What I Mean by 'Poetry' Seen in a Print

Stark pines stalk-thin on craggy hills. Magnolia
leaves sheen as black snakes' backs, unweighted
with spring's blooms, white and light as snow.
Afternoon light like the half light in a closed
room. Heron in a pond, its shallow water gray
as the slate walkway that leads to a backyard hut.
Cranes, glinting like sails vanishing into fog
or low hanging clouds, flying two by two.
An old man, wearing a straw hat, droopy shorts,
his limbs twig thin, frail and weak, his shins,
elbows knobby, bends over to work in a garden
sparse with October's final roses, their petals
feathery as a bird's wings as it slowly preens.
Our scattered lives, those who wander but will
never meet. Send me greetings from where you are.
Song, this last song for you, old man, who knew
nothing, who needed to know nothing, content
to pick flowers to gather in a basket to offer
to the wife you miss. Homeland, autumn desolations,
walking beneath a cloud-ridden sky, strolling beneath
bare vines, by a wall of dry, stacked rocks. Amber
oak leaves, rust and ruby maple leaves, tumbling on
the earth. Streaks of sunlight white as limestone, chalk lines
on yellowed paper. Reeds like scratches where the ink has faded.

II

Carolina

1.

Fifty years. Yesterdays dimming like twilight,
more dark than real. Wind-blown drifts of night.

Dawn breaks over Hanging Rock so finely
I feel no need to climb its heights again.

2.

Scaling the wind scraped mountain
where the trail steepens,
shadows shaped by the sun   .
hidden behind white clouds,

I paused by a rock ledge
where maple leaves at dusk,
frost-blushed scarlet,
burned bolder than camellia in spring.

3.

A long country highway of oriole, robin songs,
its canopy greenest at dawn,
a crossroads town with hills for walls,
cigarette posters, keen breezes.

Of its one hundred counties'
thousand backwoods churches,
how many steeples tower
above noon's haze of drizzling rain?

4.

Incised in thick moss, a pit that's stolen
its red from a twilight sky.

Later, gray clouds shadow a shadeless window
while a rising moon shines upon shingles.

5.

Faraway mountains,
hills shrouded in mist,
moonlight struggling to swim
in a churning river.

Why is he distant tonight,
so handsome, so good?
Night floods woods.
A creek flows, drowning, into a lake.

6.

I've dallied all day by a brook.
Sunset's a tawny yellow.
A fatality called autumn arrives.
See my sparse white hair?

I've trusted thunderstorms
to clear air, settle dust,
hide August's traces.
A bullfinch sings me northward.

7.

Boys keep tugging at my pants' legs, taunting,
"Why do you take so long to go home?"

I, who watched in the mirror over many lost years
the slow fading away of all I was scared of.

Ringed Scales of a Snake

1.

Note how dark it is northward: the headlands,
Tam's summit, more obscure than night, drifting

like gathering clouds weighed down by sky,
shifting like boulders more massive than mountains

invisible until, like ink on black paper,
darkness spills upon darkness, soaking in.

2.

The Pacific is thundering, its waves breaking
loud as a cascade in the heights of the Sierra

where, trailside, watching rhododendron
petals swirl in a whirlpool of bubbles and foam

he dreamed of flowing like a flower downstream
to drown in the ocean three hundred miles away.

3.

Barely visible, white water churns as far
out as the horizon. No rain. More drought.

A man walking behind him clicks on
his flashlight. Three times his height,

his shadow falls where darkness
leaves nothing to hide in.

4.

Scattered lights on the sea, by shoreline
and cliffs. Improvisatory, transient,

a container ship's lit portholes,
crabbers' lanterns hung from masts

glow dim as candlelight. A flickering
to form a constellation from. To give a name to.

5.

Say: Moth dust. Waxwing's feathers. Ringed scales
of a snake. Kingbird's beak. Crockery shards.

Door bolt. Bear tooth. Mermaid's seaweed
hair. Twirling seeds. Grape pips. Flowering plum.

Night blinded things, lined up like stars. Each a sign.
Phosphorescent rocks. Pine stand. A dam's open sluice.

6.

Not where he walks, but how, sand sinking
beneath his feet, tide erasing his footprints,

dawn never to shine again, morning
arriving as night: sky, earth, sea

not freed into day but chained
like a lake in Siberian winter.

7.

No moon. No emptiness in its stead. No visible
pit in the sky. Solace comes in breeze's

kindness, the play of water in tide pools,
their starless gleaming slick as black silk,

incandescent, the blackened azure sky.
A crevasse between dunes, a streetlight blinking.

8.

To dwell in enlightenment and suspect day.
To know woods, hills, a river, eyes lit

by the visible, what illuminates them. Or to walk
on a morning darker than midnight,

the distance between them the words
he uses to plot their historical traces.

9.

To envision night flightless as a gimp bird.
Ink-dark water, barren hills, mountains

barred like a wrought iron gate. To see
shadows scattering. Waves crashing, swash

flowing, the coast jagged, sword-tip sharp.
To hear cliffs slowly shattering. Beseeching all.

10.

Night like a mountain twice climbed,
a river crossed, its dangerous portage.

Night like a way to a place elsewhere lost,
an unmanned boat drifting at sea.

Night like the wildness inside you, tendril
and vines thriving by clinging to rock face.

A Letter

1.

A black pearl sky. Dark clouds, drifting.
A waning moon like lanterns in rain.

Dawn, when it comes, like autumn's
last light, a wind sharp as winter's.

At noon, I resume my exile, weak
as a newborn's my arms my only oarsman.

The water winds upriver between rock face cliffs
like a snake slithering through dew-wet grass.

You wait for me where mountain peaks are
white as your hair. Why dress in fine raiments?

Your letters sound a thousand sighs. Days end
where cranes begin their longest journey.

The past is a leaf fast drifting toward a waterfall,
a dog tied to a stake, a servant's well-kept lies.

2.

No more springtime bird-calls.
No more thoughts of my brothers.

No more gardenias blooming,
the perfume my mother wore for parties.

The Yadkin no longer flows steady and green
with the clarity of a thousand new streams.

Dawn-tinged pink clouds float in the sky,
lost as the songs of a hundred years.

3.

I look far off at Tamalpais' summit.
Pacific's tides wash smoke ash from shoreline.

To debate like philosophers with hills charred by fire.
To argue with wilderness how all is not right.

If only I knew why life reads like bad fiction.
If only I knew why I pursued the wrong way.

4.

I tell myself stories of lakes and streams,
how dreams resemble the mist in clouds.

Fall's first rain blows sand off the dunes
like dust from the world. It drenches my clothes.

So many decades since we all parted, friends,
lovers. I work at my desk like a wife at her loom.

5.

I think a lot about my early youth
when I read books in unhoed fields.

Before I knew it, those days ended.
I click on the light over my bed.

I've broken my ties with red clay,
with people who talked and knew nothing.

6.

Last night, in a story I made up to help me sleep,
I returned home to see my best friend.

I called. He turned his head to look with the eyes
of a man who had never known me. Dead

eyes. Wasp's waists. Stork's knees.
The rhythms of poetry still possess things.

Flowers scatter. Birds fly off. Tears
fall. And Paul no longer beside me.

7.

To live is a fantasy, a tale of Pine Cone Mountain.
I lie alone behind dunes, their fissures folded like cliffs.

It is dark this side of the ocean.
Why is the mind near life's end not freer of clamor?

For years I have dreamed of a stone bridge,
a wet, twisting path, a rust-colored pond.

Of a city whose buildings were the colors
of crags in old hills. What years remain?

Some valleys are more beautiful the deeper
you enter. I grow older and do what I please.

The trees on Pine Cone Mountain grow darker the brighter
the sun. The things we can't say, unstained.

Why do people want to be better? I am the letter
I never could write you, the story I left you untold.

The End of His Story

1.

A two hour storm in the middle
of the night. From the west, winds

break like waves against windows
and doors. I can't rest, possessed

by a spirit that claims my sleep,
no phantom but the fulfillment

of a wish taking form,
reborn in a wilderness,

old woods restored by dreaming,
by a storm that won't relent.

2.

Two boys playing, cavorting like fools,
breaking rules, exploring caves,

crevasses, animals' tracks,
no grown-up's cares, a peace

they're not aware of. Below
leaf-hidden skies, they speak in spells.

3.

Shimmering pleats of light,
geese, raccoons, jays gracing

the lake where they swim,
the banks they loll on.

A forest of loblolly pine,
ash, oak, hickory, spruce,

ivy, kudzu, honeysuckle,
owls, snakes, mosquitoes, squirrels.

Two boys embraced by green,
entangled in vines, creeping ivy,

bark, burls, gnarled branches
scary, staring at them,

little children fogging
the panes of bedroom windows

wanting back the lives they lost
too long ago to remember.

4.

Mid-day, eating hickory nuts
cracked open with rocks,

hunched, crouched, drinking water
flowing over pebbles

crystalline as the new dimes
they toss in to recover,

silvery minnows in sunlight,
as they pee into the stream

or on piles of rotting leaves,
the sound of their piss like rain

falling on the tarpaper roof
of Ronnie's father's backyard barn.

5.

Just before sunset, trekking home,
a downpour on its way, roaming,

not rushing since no one's
looking for them,

not yet, slowly wandering back,
nine year old boys holding hands,

their fingers entwined, woven
like yarn in a sweater,

webs spiders weave among leaves
of a willow, reed-thin twigs

of bushes seeking light, knit
together in one leafy shrub.

6.

There's a ring round the moon that shines
on the pup tent they've pitched

beside Ravens Creek, clouds scattering
black and massive as floating mountains.

The constellation of the Great Bear
sets over the lake, a fire from kindling

burning as both dance to its flames
naked as pagans, muttering prayers

to its heat, its flickering light,
too drowsy to admit how tired they are,

creeping into the tent whose flaps
they leave open, untied, letting the night

do what it likes, the air, earth so full,
of cries, mournful sounds, nothing's

asleep, the summer white, encircled
moon drying their unshed tears.

7.

You, I, each our father's only son,
swearing to live forever in woods.

To be done with it all. This, my way of
saying it, my dream of seeing it through.

8.

Wild child, lost, first friend,
if dreaming is a prayer

to eternal summer,
to a boundless wilderness

best found at night, then,
when you wake to the sun,

night's winds dying, do not
go, do not return home

emptied handed. Come. You grieve
for want of knowing. Touch this tree.

9.

My hair's whiter by first light. A leaf
from a hedge tumbles onto the deck.

Old age sneaks in. I've nothing to do
with its violations. Shadows aslant,

the moon sinks lower. Desolate winter.
Slow, stormy nights. I sleep strolling

through pine, under grass-green canopies,
by sloping hills, golden ridge tops,

a lake, creek, dawn-lit untilled field,
an ancient oak misted with hoarfrost.

I am a boy ages older than I am
who died at ten of polio.

I am the end of his story. I am
the forest his memory's wooded.

The Last Clouds of Summer

1.

White the last clouds of summer,
white, white, the white inside me.

The pebbles in the seaward stream are white
as chalk, the sun's light bent toward fall.

No one lives more than once. What is man at the end
but a bare, rocky hill where weeds uneasily grow?

2.

The garden withers. The water in my glass
sparkles like October. A neighbor plays his guitar.

You say the sky today is so blue it will stay
blue forever. How much longer might we live?

A man squats on a dune and cries, terrified.
You wonder at the dawn, how it colors my glass.

3.

Evening. Flowers, leaves breathe out fragrantly.
A cat sneaks out of the shrubbery.

Birds flee, perching on wires, roof tops.
One sings from a bush, reedy, flute-sweet.

The earth, the sand below my feet, is ready
for sleep. Sings to it in their shared language.

4.

Autumn mists float over Chain of Lakes.
Frost coats the reeds, weeds, and grasses.

Rest here a while, where we first met.
A cold like stones weighs on my heart.

Blue mists of night, like fire's hottest flames.
White mists like ice, the sun as it rises.

5.

If only I knew a land where I might set up
a new house. Where you might follow me.

If only I knew a land where I might find
peace. No nightmares of lice or rats infesting things.

The vermin of time. A house, safe, but dark as a cave,
without windows or doors. A house safe as a palace.

6.

Friends gather in a pavilion of green and white porcelain.
A bridge, built from ancient timber, arches its back

over a pond like a riled cat, a dancer at his exercise.
People beautifully dressed, smiling, drinking,

talking of worlds soon faint as ghosts. And you, alone
as you cross the bridge, mirrored by a pool moon-full.

7.

A handsome boy walks out of the surf onto the shore.
More handsome boys shine in sharp sunlight.

Young men run through the park, through its trees
and green meadows, faster than cars,

faster than clocks run seconds past us. Beach and sea caressing
their beauty, the gleam in their eyes less glowing than mine.

8.

Wonderful sleep, the way winter sneaks in overnight.
To wake to day still drunk, like a man who has finished his bottle,

smashed it on rocks when he is through, the last
dropped swallowed. Like dark swallowed by starlight.

Like hours devoured by dreaming. (I have lied to you,
my darling.) Like fantasies consumed by my heart.

9.

I'm waiting for my friend. Why did he depart before me?
Twilight is an umber color or the red of dying embers.

Sing of rivers. Sing of mountains. Of the beloved earth,
of life, precious life. Of the journey that saves us.

You who have gone there, seen what I can't yet see, tell me
of death. How it finds with its torches lost paintings in caves.

10.

A white-haired monk, poling his skiff, recites his goodbyes.
Birds chirp a reply. The river he travels on is eternity,

illusionless change, his poem implies. The hills through which
its shallows twist are shaded by pine, bay, and ash, bleak woods,

an old oak forest slight sun shines in. To follow upstream
past dreams into trees, toward night. To be what none can know.

11.

Say a horse gallops near you. Pretend it and its rider
pause beside you. Say white clouds pass over head
in a sky so piercingly clear you could expire that day.

Imagine it is the last time you'll meet each other.
So you embrace. Where is he going,
riding far away on his horse if not to war?

Suppose it is love you feel or some abiding passion.
Reticence, absence, the glimmer of half light,
the surety that hides in the sunniest mornings.

12.

A heavy rain ends in silence. In solitude.
Runoff trickles into a crystalline stream,
flows through corn fields clear to the woods.

Autumn resounds with the colors of trees.
Mourning fades into November skies. A cold sun
settles over distant peaks like a wildfire

burning grasses on their ridges. I was born
of rock and pine. I learned to live in a city where a night
like a backwood church's bell might call down heaven.

God's Own Country

1.

Evenings they watch over sheep in the hills, moor-like
in their stony bareness. Mornings they watch over sheep.

Twilight, ordinary goodbyes, the way
of all life. Darkness like the kindness of labor.

Seek from this wind-shorn, stark, rapt country
what God sees in ill-shaped rock walls and pasture.

2.

Who live apart, overlooking valleys, wild lands,
lights from faraway cottages, scattered villages.

Shepherds, masters of solitude, quietly eating
by a fire their breakfast of soup and noodles.

In the sheepfold, a lamb in the fleece of another
suckles at the teats of the dead lamb's mother.

3.

Thistles, nettles, yellow petaled gorse, harbingers
of spring. Dawn clouds flame-singed by sunlight.

Mist lingers over the lower fields. They lie on straw
against a stone wall, haltingly talking of unspoken things.

Of unsaid sorrows past. A race up a hill, one pursuing
the other. To the heights of the world, its stilled, harsh beauty.

4.

Winds on a late autumn night, scattering dust
and twigs. The sound of mourning through chinks

in the near ruins of an ancient, one room cottage,
a soughing like a mother's who has lost her son,

a father's who has lost his boy. The great
clarity of love, of hands pressed to a man's chest,

his thigh, of the ardor that rises in the earthy musk,
the raw savor of sweating, unwashed flesh.

5.

Never idleness, never rest. Silence deepening,
well-like, the days unfolding in hesitant spring.

A pond, graceful of itself, alone, still cold with winter's chill.
Trees' slight branches, a green canopy protective

as slate roofs. They leap in, jump out quickly
in the eternity of children playing beneath new leaves.

6.

Down below, in a small town bar, Johnny offers
Gheorghe a beer. Asks if he is leaving, where he is going.

Has their work come to nothing, only more suffering?
Should he set out, vanish, all doubts might end

in his feeding bleating sheep, lowing cows, raking, mucking,
hoeing, plowing the earth, the ground as starved as he is for seed.

7.

Smoldering cook fires. Empty, sparse tree groves.
He is through with struggling for a place in the human world.

The last of his youth like a wilderness, like a lamb, cheated
of life, lying on its side smeared by filth from afterbirth and barn.

Not knowing how to care. Not knowing how to bare it.
Kicking it to hurt it, to deny God the right to his stillborn country.

8.

Dark eyed with love. Possessed by the reticence
of shadows that follow you, the demons

who muffle your heart. Shut the gate. Let
no sheep or steer escape. You, who would hurry

out to welcome him back, what have you not
buried inside you? Memory is a wild bird

in search of a cage. Return to your bramble-, brushbound
house. Lock all doors against the threat of kindness.

9.

I want you to stay. It is summer passing by our way house. Days,
the gentle green of willows, birches, alder by streams,

hills, their fields lovely, though spare as moorlands, farewells over.
We two are rain in midday sunlight, sheep grazing in peace.

Look. The caravan you lived in is being towed away. Come into
my room. Stay. What is home but the plenty of need?

It is the season for farming. Life ensuing, never ending, you, like moonlight
asleep on our bed and I, safe as the stones in the wall where you piled them.

The Three Great Griefs

All through the village, by water's strict
edges, people suffer. The age of Three
Great Griefs promises no end. Joy
darkens eyes with its shadows of regret.
Young, we move through time slowly.
Old, we watch ourselves decay faster
than dreams play their seductive music,
the tricks of memory. Sudden as black
clouds shadow people from the sea,
they leap into their graves, yet will not
rest there. Chant the rules of sorrow
each night for me. A wren passes over
a backyard garden. A martin's sapphire
plumage dazzles at a window. Tomorrow
it comes, soon enough. Let us stay till tomorrow.

An Apple

As if intent on something,
all day I watch
through a window
white clouds growing.
It is spring.
Who doesn't appreciate
a happy dream?
My white, shaggy hair
hangs down,
my face is unshaven,
my emerald irises
smile at mysteries,
my parched, pink lips,
pinched and old, smack
like flapping fish as I gnaw an apple.

A Mirror

The mind is a mirror.
Polish it. Do not
let dust collect.
Do not mistake
the face you see for it.
The tree of dreams
has no roots or boughs,
its door has no handle
to open it with,
its window no latch
to lock it with.
The only glass
a mirror needs
to reflect your soul
is transparency.
Polish it, I say. Wipe it
clean of steam from your breath.

Plato

1.

Beaches are good places to seek silence,
though waves crack like ice floes
breaking. Near sunset,
winds return with a deliberate violence,

like a grief one knows that never goes
away. Crumbling, destitute, wet
to the core, the seawall's
failing. A kitesurfer flies over the sea

where white caps leap far as the horizon.
A swimmer in a wetsuit crawls
out of the surf, exhausted.
Crows and gulls scurry,

caw or shriek as if mimicking a dirge.
Pounding waves surge
past the highway, sand-slicked,
sticky with seaweed. Why,

like the stillness abiding inside terror,
does all go quiet
when you sigh, in breathless ululation
at the wonder of it, the muted abstention

of sense as if nothing belongs to time
now the other world's begun
and nothing, no one,
knows how to praise life in the ways of the sublime.

2.

A boy who has lost the good of his mind
but not his gaiety,
dances on a dune as if blind
to the tragedy his eyes see

clearly, the ghosts he evokes of,
oh, I don't know, some love
he once knew and lost
to the sea and its heaving waters.

3.

If time's most painful powers are yet to come,
leave with me. Let us return home.
Seek comfort in heron, egret, snake,
plaited reeds and ferns, mist off the lake,

clouds dividing, re-gathering, black,
steely gray, battered, yet sheen
as satin or the smoke-stack-
ashen of velvet, creeks a phosphorescent green.

Let the great rain again flood farms,
pour down on our town. And on you
and me getting wetter, too,
since the storm harms

nothing important. Spillway. Bird wing.
Water lily. Oak tree. The world
as we knew it swirled
up in the beauty and thrill of lightning

on a summer afternoon, the throbbing air,
thunderbolts, rushing water,
gale-like winds: something of despair
in it, I suppose, but you and I were never happier.

4

Take care of your ghosts, I'm told. Offer them
common pleasures. They float over
the world wanting back in. At the beach,
a steel-like smell stings the air.

Salt dust encrusts sand, pebbles, rocks,
shards of crabs' shells. A crow pecks
at a fish's gutted, bony carcass.
A man in waders deftly casts his line.

Spray from high waves hovers over
the beach, gushes past walls,
splashes onto streets. Seawater
spouts from car tires as off boats' hulls.

A rust- and sulfur-colored foam
drifts, rolling like tumbleweed
across the sand, along the dunes,
wherever breezes blow it. The madness,

the fit of humanity is in the wind
as it grows fiercer once night darkens
enough for us to sleep before the storm,
like the coming of peace, passes silently westward.

5.

At first light, some clouds are white like petals
of bay laurel, white like an old woman's hair,
like the eyes of a boy as he stares
at a bronze bird, at antique drinking vessels

in a museum, or the feathery white of dandelion
threads. Others are gray like ships beneath seas,
like wolf fur, chips in gravel pits, rain drops on stone,
faded linen, scabbards, or massive sheaves

of barn-stored grains shadowed from sunlight.
A few are black as fungus, cooled magma, onyx,
tar from pine rich with resin, ravens in flight
frightened by the morning, or as the river Styx

must be to carry us to our doom, I guess. At dawn,
they loom over a storm-endangered ocean
as if all the world were burning, the smoke drawn
heavenward like this morning's clouds, in premonition

of its ending, fires dampened, smoldering, or freshly lit
yet billowing, flowering, contracting, drifting,
through a sky whose sublimity we submit
to, the awe we yield to willingly, if devotion means anything.

6.

A metaphysics of mist,
the moon glowing
like a candle behind a scrim,
surpassing streetlights, hooded and dim.

A restless sea beats against
a craggy cement barrier
near where smoke from
a fire on the beach mixes with the drizzle.

Raccoons squabble behind
a wind-bowed silhouette
of pine as a frail man with a cane
slowly clicks by unseen on the sidewalk.

A raven or a creature as hungry
scrounges through
a trash can. Coyotes howl
in the distant recesses of the fog.

Everything invisible is clearer only if
left unspoken, silent
as this evening's whiteout in which
all the words one's said or written might vanish

into the bitterly cold, final embrace of cerecloth,
thought's cloak, the moon masked,
veiled too, haloed by mist as it sets, the heavens safe to stare at
until the blinding sun of Plato's Ideas burns through its clouds tomorrow.

Afterword

In a note at the end of *A Last Hike In*, I wrote that it would be my last full length book, yet here is another one. I do not think of *A Last Hike In* and *A Last Look Back* as separate books, however, but as one book in two volumes, each complementary to the other, Janus-faced in the important sense, as if trekking deeper into the mystery of what Keats called "the old oak Forest" were inseparable from the proddings of memory, reminding me of a few of the old, similar journeys I'd already made along the way, offering images and thoughts from the past that rhyme with the present and its presentiments of the future.

My husband and I have lived close to the Pacific for fifteen years. For several years now, first because of the pandemic, then because of old age's taking its various, inevitable tolls, this place we dwell in by the Pacific has been the sole scene of my wanderings, seen in its endless changes while also evoking fragments from my past, real and imaginary, as I looked and watched and thought about both worlds daily, the two, now and then, simultaneously before me in the mind's uncanny moments of apprehension.

This second part of my two last "Lasts," like the first, is for Atticus Carr and the life we've shared for over thirty seven years. When I am thirsty, he brings me water.

Milton Keynes UK
Ingram Content Group UK Ltd.
UKHW010732231023
431165UK00003B/157